WORLD WAR II

AIR FORCES OF WORLD WAR II

Mike Taylor

Visit us at
www.abdopub.com

Published by Abdo Publishing Company, 4940 Viking Drive, Edina, MN 55435.
Copyright ©1998 by Abdo Consulting Group, Inc. International copyrights
reserved in all countries. No part of this book may be reproduced in any form
without written permission from the publisher.

Printed in the United States.

Interior Graphic Design: John Hamilton
Cover Design: MacLean & Tuminelly
Contributing Editors: John Hamilton; Alan Gergen; Morgan Hughes
Cover photo: Digital Stock
Interior photos: Digital Stock, page 3
               AP/Wide World Photos, pages 13, 27
               Corbis, pages 1, 4-10, 12, 14, 15, 21, 22, 24-26, 28

Sources: Ambrose, Stephen E. *American Heritage New History of World War II.*
New York: Penguin Books, 1997. Jablonski, Edward. *Flying Fortress.* New York:
Doubleday, 1965. Piekalkiewicz, Janusz. *The Air War.* Poole/Dorset: Blandford
Press, 1978. Snyder, Lois L. *The War: A Concise History, 1939-1945.* New York:
Simon & Schuster, 1960.

Library of Congress Cataloging–in–Publication Data

Taylor, Mike, 1965-
   Air forces of World War II / Mike Taylor
      p. cm. — (World War II)
   Includes index.
   Summary: Describes the different airplanes used by the air forces in World
War II and the military strategies that led to the defeat of the Axis powers.
   ISBN 1-56239-806-7
   1. World War, 1939-1945—Aerial operations—Juvenile literature. [1. World
War, 1939-1945—Aerial operations. 2. Airplanes, Military] I. Title. II. Series:
World War II (Edina, Minn.)
D785.T39 1998
940.54 '49—dc21   98-2914
                                        CIP
                                        AC

CONTENTS

Pilots on an F6F Hellcat on board the USS *Lexington*.

INTRODUCTION

A squadron of Spitfires takes off, heading for battle over the English Channel.

World War II began in September, 1939, when Germany, led by Adolf Hitler, attacked and conquered Poland in a two-week battle. Great Britain and France both pledged to assist Poland and declared war on Germany immediately. Japan, Germany's ally, attacked the United States of America at Pearl Harbor on December 7, 1941. The United States soon entered the war against Germany and Japan.

The world was divided into two great alliances. Germany, Italy, and Japan together were called the Axis powers. Great Britain, the United States, the Soviet Union, and many smaller nations together were called the Allied powers.

The Allies finally won the war in 1945. The great Allied air forces were very important to the victory. British fighter planes, the famous "Spitfires" and "Hurricanes," shot down German bombers by the hundreds in the dogfights of the Battle of Britain. B-17 bombers from the United States, nicknamed "Flying Fortresses" for their great size, released thousands of bombs over German cities night after night.

Yet the Axis powers had high-quality airplanes and heroic pilots as well. Junkers Ju87 dive bombers, called "Stukas," could hit their targets with deadly accuracy. The Germans used them to terrorize European cities throughout the war. And the speedy Japanese "Zero" was surely one of the best short-range fighter planes in the war.

The propeller of an American P-51 Mustang fighter.

THE GERMAN LUFTWAFFE

A formation of Heinkel He111 bombers.

At the beginning of the war, Germany had the newest and most powerful air force, called the "Luftwaffe." The best of Germany's planes was the Messerschmitt Bf109 fighter. With a 2,000-horsepower engine, the Bf109 flew at least 100 miles per hour (161 kph) faster than its opponents at the beginning of the war, nearly 300 mph (483 kph).

Germany also had very good bombers. Among the most important were the Heinkel He111 and the Dornier Do17 (called "Flying Pencils.") They could not carry many bombs (only 5,500 pounds worth (2,495 kg)) and they could not fly long-range missions. However, they were very fast.

Most famous among Germany's planes was the Junkers Ju87, the "Stuka" dive bomber. The Stuka was smaller than Germany's other bombers. However, the

Stuka could deliver bombs with pinpoint accuracy even on a target as small as an enemy tank or truck.

Enemy soldiers and civilians dreaded the Stuka dive bomber. The Stuka was fitted with a siren that screamed loudly as it swooped down from the sky. The screeching siren was loud enough to make every soldier in the area fear that the bomb was aimed at him personally!

Germany's fleet of small, fast fighters and dive bombers was perfectly suited to the *Blitzkrieg* style of warfare. *Blitzkrieg* means "lightning warfare" in the German language. The Germans hoped to win quick battles with small, fast tanks. The job of the Messerschmitts and Stukas was to terrorize the enemy soldiers and destroy the roads and railways so that they could be surrounded by the German army. Meanwhile, specially trained German commandos parachuted from Junkers Ju52 cargo planes for special missions.

A Junkers Ju87 Stuka dive bomber.

The *Blitzkrieg* worked very well during the first year of the war. Germany easily defeated Poland, Denmark, Norway, and France in quick *Blitzkrieg* battles.

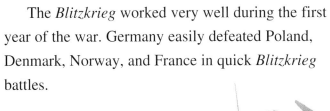

Indeed, the Germans became quite creative. In May 1941, the Luftwaffe attacked the great fortress of Eben Emael in Belgium. The fort was highly modern, armed with anti-aircraft guns and constructed from steel and concrete. Most military experts thought it could not be captured. German commando pilots flew nine-man glider airplanes onto Eben Emael's roof. The silent gliders allowed the Germans to surprise the Belgian defenders completely. The group of German commandos dynamited through the concrete and captured the great fort within 24 hours.

Dornier Do17 bombers on a mission over London, England.

Perhaps because of these quick successes, the Germans became too confident in the Luftwaffe and did nothing to develop new airplanes. Later in the war, the *Blitzkrieg* style did not work as well when German tanks were fighting far from home. Fuel and landing strips were scarce. The Messerschmitts and Stukas were no longer effective, and Germany had never developed a long-range bomber that could fly all the way from Germany to its many "fronts."

A long-range bomber might have helped Germany to defeat Great Britain. Instead, the Luftwaffe squandered the precious Messerschmitts and Stukas recklessly in the Battle of Britain.

A British Spitfire tries to shoot down a Heinkel He111 bomber.

THE BATTLE OF BRITAIN

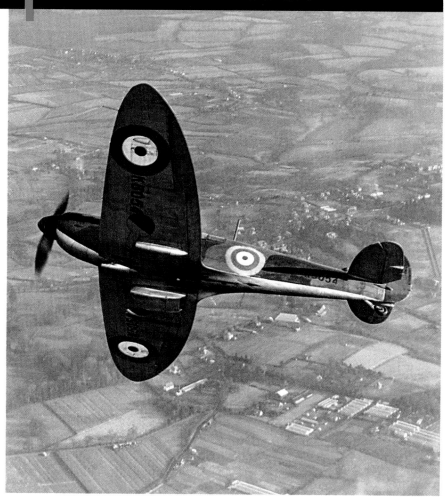

A Spitfire begins a barrel roll in the skies over England.

Although Great Britain was respected most for its great navy, its air force was very important as well. The British Royal Air Force (R.A.F.) was smaller than the German Luftwaffe. However, it possessed very good equipment.

Before the war, foresighted British leaders had installed along the British coast a brand new technology called radar. A radar unit can determine the location of objects by bouncing sound waves off of them. By measuring the time it takes for the wave to return, radar operators can determine how fast the object is moving and in which direction. With radar, the British could predict German attacks and order their own fighter planes into the air to intercept the Germans before they even reached British territory.

British fighter airplanes, the famous Spitfires and Hurricanes, were the best in Europe. Powered by huge Rolls Royce engines, these fast fighters were perfect for chasing down the German attackers over the English Channel before they reached British territory. They were made even faster yet by the invention of a new adjustable propeller called the Havilland propeller.

The German attack finally came in July 1940, and then intensified in August. Adolf Hitler's plan was to destroy the R.A.F. so that the German army could cross the channel safely on ships. Therefore, Hitler concentrated on bombing R.A.F. airfields and radar units. The German bombers could cross the channel to England and return easily, even with their small fuel tanks. The Messerschmitt fighters, however, had a much shorter range and could not escort the bombers all the way to England and back. Many Messerschmitts went down in the channel after running out of fuel. German floatplanes swooped in and rescued the pilots, since trained pilots were as precious as the airplanes themselves.

At the start, the R.A.F. was outnumbered in every category of aircraft. Even though the Hurricanes and Spitfires shot down German bombers by the hundreds,

A British R.A.F. Spitfire fighter plane.

A squadron of Hurricanes.

the danger was that Britain would run out of fighter planes before the Germans ran out of bombers. In one day, on August 12, 1940 (known as "Eagle Day"), the British shot down 65 German planes, enough to damage the Luftwaffe very seriously. However, three days later, the British lost 34 planes themselves. Experienced pilots became scarce as well. Many pilots had no experience at all. The British estimated that a new pilot had a 50 percent chance of being shot down on his first flight!

Hitler's commander of the Luftwaffe, Hermann Göring, planned the greatest attack on the city of London for September 15, 1940. The Germans sent hundreds of airplanes toward London. Many succeeded in hitting their targets, and many London civilians were killed. However, at the end of the day, the R.A.F. had shot down more than 60 German planes. Of these, 35 were bombers, leaving Germany with less than 250 bombers remaining. By 1940, Great Britain's factories had built more than 15,000 war planes. After Germany's surprise defeat on September 15, Hitler postponed further action into Britain.

A section of London lies in ruins after a German bombing run.

 13

THE JAPANESE EMPIRE

A Mitsubishi A6M Zero fighter.

The Japanese Empire joined the Axis powers shortly before the war began. Japanese leaders hoped to expand the Japanese Empire to the south, to capture the Philippine Islands from the United States. Finally, in 1941, the United States imposed an oil embargo on Japan. This meant that Japan could no longer purchase oil and fuel.

Like Germany, Japan had a very modern air force. Japan's air force also concentrated on high-performance fighter planes and small bombers.

The Mitsubishi factories built many of Japan's most important planes, including the famous Mitsubishi A6M fighter, nicknamed the "Zero" by the United States. The Zero was very fast, with top speeds up to 350 mph (563 kph). It was also the most maneuverable plane in the war. American and British pilots considered a dogfight with a Japanese Zero to be futile, and avoided direct confrontation.

Equally famous was the Aichi D3 dive bomber, nicknamed the "Val." Like the German Stuka dive bomber, the Val was not fast, and did not have a long range. Nor could it carry heavy bombs. However, it was deadly accurate and well suited to the style of fighting preferred by Japanese generals. Also important was the Nakajima torpedo plane, nicknamed the "Kate," which could deliver a heavy torpedo with great accuracy.

A Kate torpedo plane goes down in flames.

The greatest victory of the Japanese air force was its successful surprise attack on the American fleet at Pearl Harbor in Hawaii. The Japanese fleet that attacked Pearl Harbor included six aircraft carriers. Each carried between 60 and 70 planes, mostly Zeroes, Vals, and Kates. On the morning of December 7, 1941, the Japanese fleet moved within range.

The Zeroes were assigned the task of destroying American fighter planes as they tried to protect the ships. In fact, the Zeroes were able to destroy most American planes before they even left the ground because the American pilots were not prepared.

Meanwhile, swarms of Val dive bombers attacked the American ships. The attack was made easier by the fact that the Americans had all of their massive battleships tied up along "Battleship Row" in the port. This made them easy targets for the dive bombers.

Japanese torpedoes did the most damage, however. The torpedoes were launched from "midget"

Planes take off from a Japanese aircraft carrier on their way to Pearl Harbor.

submarines and Kate torpedo planes. They were much larger than conventional bombs. An accurate hit could sink a battleship. The *Arizona*, one of the prized battleships in the U.S. fleet, was hit perfectly, splitting the ship in two. It sank immediately.

The aftermath of the Pearl Harbor attack.

It soon became clear that the attack was an overwhelming victory for Japan. The Japanese force sank or damaged several battleships, cruisers, and destroyers. Nearly 200 American planes were destroyed and another 100 planes were badly damaged. Most importantly, 2,403 Americans were killed, and another 1,100 wounded. By contrast, Japan lost only 29 planes and 5 midget submarines, along with the men aboard.

In the long run, however, the Japanese surprise attack on Pearl Harbor proved to be a mistake. The United States proved it could easily replace ships and planes faster than the Japanese could destroy them. Japanese leaders were proud that their factories could produce as many as 5,000 new planes in 1941, more than either Germany or Great Britain. The United States, on the other hand, amazed the world by producing 20,000 new planes in that same year!

1939 *September*: Battle of Poland. German *Blitzkrieg* overwhelms Poland with high-speed tanks and aircraft. The Battle of Poland was the beginning of World War II.

November 1939—May 1940: The Phony War. Britain and France declare war on Germany, but the fight doesn't start until May 1940.

1940 *August—September:* Battle of Britain. Britain uses newly invented radar units and fighter airplanes to intercept German bombers. The Battle of Britain was the largest air battle in World War II.

1941 *December 7:* Surprise attack on Pearl Harbor. Japanese aircraft carriers stage successful surprise attack and destroy much of the American fleet at Pearl Harbor in Hawaii. Because the Japanese used strict radio silence, it was impossible for the Americans to intercept messages and predict the attack.

1942 *June:* Battle of Midway. One of the greatest battles among aircraft carriers. Japanese aircraft carriers attack, but the Americans are prepared and win the battle decisively. The Americans sink four Japanese aircraft carriers. The Japanese sink one American carrier, the *Yorktown*.

1942 *August 7:* Battle of Guadalcanal. U.S. Marines use landing craft to invade and capture this important island from the Japanese.

1942-43 *Winter:* Battle of Stalingrad. Germans and Soviets engage in street-to-street and building-to-building battle for the Soviet city of Stalingrad. Small machine guns were very important to this style of fighting. In February 1943 the surviving Germans ran out of ammunition and supplies and were forced to surrender. German and Russian casualties totalled nearly 500,000 men.

1944 *June 6:* D-Day. Allied forces use hundreds of small landing craft to attack the beaches of northern France. The Allies landed so many soldiers in this way that they eventually liberated Paris and pushed the Germans out of France.

1945 *May 8:* V-E Day. Victory in Europe! The Germans surrender to American General Dwight D. Eisenhower.

1945 *August 6:* Hiroshima. American bomber *Enola Gay* drops an atomic bomb on the Japanese city of Hiroshima. Around 130,000 Japanese civilians are killed or wounded. Three days later, on August 9, another atomic bomb is dropped on the city of Nagasaki.

1945 *August 14:* Japanese surrender. Japan surrenders to the Allies after witnessing the terrible destruction in the cities of Hiroshima and Nagasaki. The surrender documents are signed by Japanese representatives aboard the USS *Missouri*.

A U.S. Liberator bomber flies over a pair of P-40 Warhawks.

Two of the best U.S. fighters, especially during the first half of the war, were the Curtiss P-40 "Warhawk" and the Grumman F4F "Wildcat." Both were faster than the Japanese Zero, with maximum speeds over 350 mph (563 kph). Both, however, were heavier and less maneuverable than the Zero. Indeed, pilots avoided close dogfights with the Japanese Zeroes, and tried instead to hit them from a distance.

The American SBD "Dauntless" dive bomber was every bit as effective as the Japanese Val. Like the other American planes, the Dauntless was heavier than its Japanese counterpart. But it was stronger, faster, and carried twice the bombing payload.

The Battle of Midway, in June 1942, proved the value of the Dauntless dive bombers and the Wildcat fighters. Like the Battle of Britain, the Battle of

Midway was fought mostly over water and mostly by fighters and dive bombers. Here, though, the majority of the aircraft were stationed on aircraft carriers, and the targets were the great ships themselves.

Midway is a group of American islands located about 1,500 miles (2,414 km) northwest of Hawaii. The Japanese leaders wanted to capture the islands in

Grumman F4F Wildcats line the deck of an American aircraft carrier.

An SBD Dauntless begins a dive-bombing run.

order to make the Pacific Ocean safer for the Japanese navy. In June 1942 a huge Japanese attack fleet, including 4 aircraft carriers, 11 battleships, and more than 200 other ships, approached Midway. The Japanese hoped to overwhelm the U.S. base the way it had overwhelmed Pearl Harbor.

This time, it was the Japanese who were surprised! A large American fleet, including four aircraft carriers, was waiting north of Midway Island. On June 4, the U.S. planes, mostly Dauntless dive bombers and Wildcat fighters, concentrated their attacks on the Japanese aircraft carriers. On the carrier *Kaga* there were loose torpedoes and spilled fuel lying on the deck. Four 500-pound bombs dropped from a Dauntless bomber exploded on the flight deck of the *Kaga.* A massive fire broke out, and the *Kaga*'s bombs and torpedoes began to explode. Firefighters could not control the blaze. The *Kaga* sank three hours later. Sadly, flames trapped 800 crewmembers below deck who went down with their ship. (Just minutes earlier, 718 men went down with the *Soryu*, the largest aircraft carrier in the Japanese navy.)

In the meantime, the Japanese Vals and Zeroes had turned their fury against the American carriers. The *Yorktown* was burned, and its planes, returning from the attack, had nowhere to land. The planes tried to fly the extra distance to land on the carrier *Enterprise*, but many ran out of fuel and ditched into the sea.

Finally, late in that same day, American dive bombers attacked the Japanese carrier *Hiryu*. The *Hiryu* caught fire and was destroyed by the explosion of its own fuel and torpedoes. That night the Japanese admiral ordered the crippled fleet to retreat. The Battle of Midway was one of the greatest air battles in history, and a great victory for the United States.

An F6F Hellcat fighter on the deck of the aircraft carrier USS *Yorktown*.

STRATEGIC BOMBING CAMPAIGNS

A B-17 Flying Fortress makes a bombing run.

While the Axis powers ignored the lessons of the early war, the Allies quickly learned that they needed more long-range bombers. Long-range bombers would allow them to bomb German cities. They hoped that this would ruin Germany's factories and force the German military to surrender.

The United States produced the largest bombers in the war. The two most important were the Convair B-24 "Liberator," and the Boeing B-17 "Flying Fortress." Both had four engines, and could fly long distances carrying many bombs. In addition, Great Britain also produced an excellent bomber called the "Lancaster." The Lancaster was a four-engine model with great speed and a huge payload.

The Lancasters usually flew at night and were not very accurate. While they tried to target factories, much of the damage was done to the homes of civilian families. For example, a huge Allied bombing mission in July 1943 destroyed the port city of Hamburg. The Allies dropped thousands of fire bombs. The city's old homes, constructed mostly of wood, burned quickly. The fire was so hot that even the pavement in the street burned.

Bombs from a B-17 fall over a German target.

Meanwhile, the United States developed two new planes to finish off the German Luftwaffe. The B-17 bomber was nicknamed the Flying Fortress because of its thick armor and numerous machine guns. The B-24s and Lancasters could fly faster and carry more bombs. However, the Flying Fortress could fly much higher to avoid the German guns on the ground. Furthermore, the armor and guns of the Flying Fortress could defend it better against the German fighters.

The second new plane was the P-51 "Mustang" fighter plane. The Mustang was much faster and much more maneuverable than the British Hurricane and Spitfire. It was superior even to Germany's best Messerschmitt fighters.

Most importantly, the Mustang was equipped with a very large fuel tank mounted on its belly. This allowed it to escort the B-17 Flying Fortresses from England deep into German territory. It could defend against German fighters. Then it dropped its empty belly-tank and returned to England with the fuel stored in its wing tanks.

This combination of long-range fighters and bombers finally overwhelmed the Luftwaffe. In one

An American
P-51 Mustang
fighter.

week during February 1944, the B-17s dropped 10,000 tons of bombs on Germany, concentrating on oil refineries and railroads. Meanwhile, the Mustangs helped destroy over 4,000 German planes during February and March.

By the summer of 1944 the Luftwaffe was ruined, and German industry was in a shambles. Desperately, the Germans rushed the Messerschmitt Me262 jet fighter into production. The Me262 was the only jet aircraft to be used in the war. Flying at over 500 mph (805 kph), it was by far the best fighter in the world. However, the ruined German factories could produce only a few, and they were overwhelmed by the great numbers of Mustangs that the Allies produced.

The Allied bombers and fighters controlled the skies over Germany. The ruined factories in Germany could no longer produce enough ammunition for the soldiers at the front. The ruined oil refineries could no longer produce enough fuel for the army's tanks and trucks.

The strategic bombing of German cities greatly weakened Germany's army and hastened the end of the war. After the D-Day invasion on June 6, 1944,

Allied troops could liberate France and Germany in only one year because the Allied planes controlled the skies. Adolf Hitler, who lived in an underground bunker to avoid the constant bombing, committed suicide in despair. Germany finally surrendered to the Allies on May 7, 1945.

Strategic bombing had a similar effect in Japan. B-29 bombers destroyed Japanese fuel storage tanks, and set fires in Japanese cities just like the fires in Germany. Desperate Japanese pilots, called kamikazes, tried to crash their Zero fighters into U.S. ships. They had no fuel or ammunition left to fight in the air. Finally, on August 6 and August 9, 1945, American B-29s dropped atomic bombs on the cities of Hiroshima and Nagasaki.

These new bombs shocked the entire world with their power. Both cities were destroyed instantly by the atomic blasts. The fires that followed were so hot that they boiled water in the rivers and melted glass in homes. Hundreds of thousands of civilians were killed by the bombs. In despair at the destruction, the Japanese finally surrendered on August 14, 1945.

A Japanese kamikaze suicide plane swoops down on a U.S. warship.

CONCLUSION

There were heroes among the pilots and planes of all sides during the war. One should not forget that the German and Japanese pilots fought for their leaders as bravely and honestly as did their American and British counterparts in the great air battles of Britain and the Pacific. Fortunately, the German and Japanese leaders overlooked the importance of long-range strategic bombing until it was too late.

The crew of the American B-17 bomber "Nora."

INTERNET SITES

A-Bomb WWW Museum
http://www.csi.ad.jp/ABOMB/index.html
   This site provides readers with accurate information concerning the impact of the first atomic bomb on Hiroshima, Japan.

Black Pilots Shatter Myths
http://www.af.mil/news/features/features95/f_950216-112_95feb16.html
   This site tells of the exploits of the 332nd Fighter Group, the first all-black flying unit known as the Tuskegee Airmen.

United States Holocaust Museum
http://www.ushmm.org/
   The official Web site of the U.S. Holocaust Memorial Museum in Washington, D.C.

What Did You Do In The War, Grandma?
http://www.stg.brown.edu/projects/WWII_Women/tocCS.html
   An oral history of Rhode Island women during World War II. In this project, 17 students interviewed 36 Rhode Island women who recalled their lives in the years before, during, and after the Second World War.

World War II Commemoration
http://gi.grolier.com/wwii/wwii_mainpage.html
   To commemorate the 50th anniversary of the end of the war, Grolier Online assembled a terrific collection of World War II historical materials on the Web. Articles taken from *Encyclopedia Americana* tell the story of World War II, including biographies. Also included are combat films, photographs, a World War II history test, and links to many other sites.

These sites are subject to change. Go to your favorite search engine and type in "World War II" for more sites.

Pass It On
   World War II buffs: educate readers around the country by passing on information you've learned about World War II. Share your little-known facts and interesting stories. We want to hear from you! To get posted on the ABDO & Daughters website, E-mail us at "History@abdopub.com"

Visit the ABDO & Daughters website at www.abdopub.com

 29

GLOSSARY

The Aircraft of Nazi Germany:

Heinkel He111 and the Dornier Do17 bombers
These mid-sized bombers with two engines were fast, but could not fly long distances.

Messerschmitt Bf109 fighter
Powered by a 2,000-horsepower engine, the Bf109 could fly over 300 mph (483 kph).

Junkers Ju87 "Stuka" dive bomber
Very accurate and effective during the *Blitzkrieg* attacks. Fitted with loud, screeching sirens, the Stukas frightened the inhabitants of European cities more than it damaged them.

Messerschmitt Me262 fighter
The only jet aircraft to be used in World War II. The Me262 could easily exceed 500 mph (805 kph). Luckily, Germany could produce only a few of them.

A Stuka dive bomber.

The Aircraft of Great Britain:

Spitfire and Hurricane fighters
Both played a very important role in defending Great Britain from German invaders during the Battle of Britain. The new adjustable Havilland propellers made them more than a match for Germany's Messerschmitts.

A British Spitfire fighter.

Lancaster bomber
The Lancaster was a great long-range bomber that played the most important role in the bombing raids of Hamburg.

A Lancaster bomber.

The Aircraft of Japan:

Mitsubishi A6 fighter
Nicknamed the "Zero," this was the most effective fighter in the war. It combined great speed with amazing maneuverability. American pilots avoided the Zeros, or tried to shoot them down from a distance whenever possible.

A Zero fighter.

Aichi D3 dive bomber
Nicknamed the "Val," the D3 dive bomber was every bit as effective as the American and German dive bombers.

Nakajima torpedo plane
Nicknamed the "Kate," this torpedo plane was one of Japan's most important planes. The torpedoes were deadly accurate. The Kates did tremendous damage to the U.S. fleet during the surprise attack on Pearl Harbor.

The Aircraft of the United States:

Curtiss P-40 "Warhawk" and Grumman F4 "Wildcat" fighters
These were America's best fighters during the first half of the war. They were faster than the Japanese Zeros, but less maneuverable.

Douglas "Dauntless" dive bomber
The Dauntless was comparable in quality to the German Stuka and the Japanese Kate dive bombers. However, the U.S. could build them much faster than its enemies. The Dauntless played a key role in the Battle of Midway.

Boeing B-17 "Flying Fortress" bomber
The B-17 could not carry as many bombs as the British Lancaster bomber, but it could fly much higher and had more machine guns. This made it better suited for flying long-range missions deep into German territory.

P-51 "Mustang" fighter
This was a long-range fighter designed to escort the "Flying Fortress" bombers over Germany. It had a large fuel tank mounted on its belly.

A P-51 Mustang fighter.

INDEX